Horses:

Coloring Book V

Angela Treat Lyon

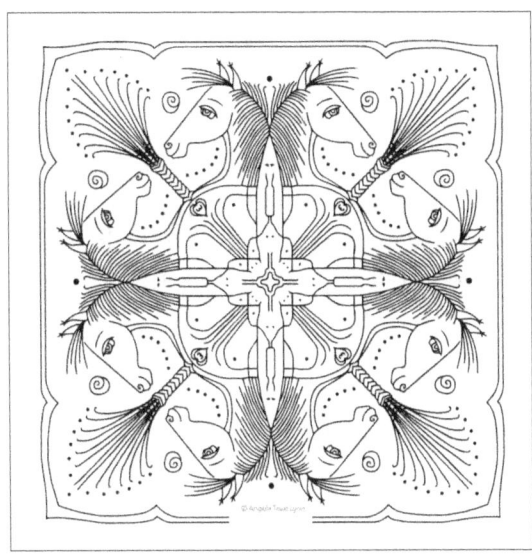
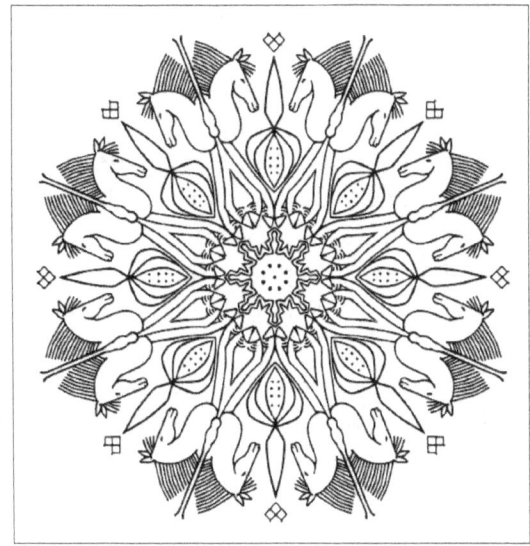
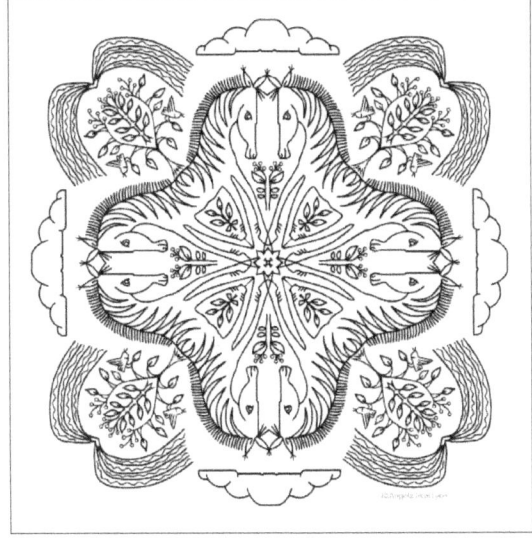
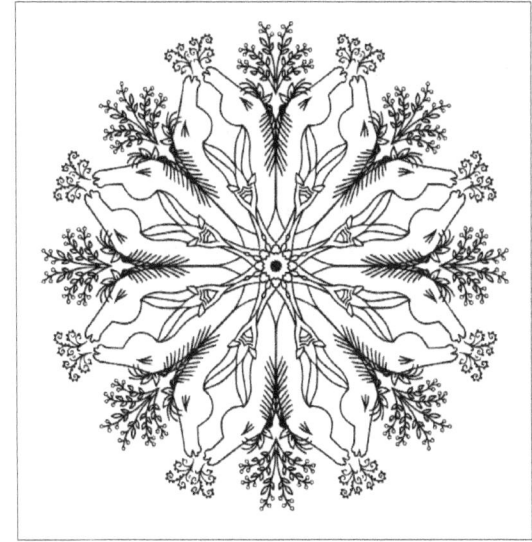

Horses:
Coloring Book V

Angela Treat Lyon

Published by Out Front Productions, LLC
Kailua, Hawaii, USA • Lyon@ColoringBookQueen.com

tISBN-13: 978-1519106131

More Books by Angela Treat Lyon: on Amazon.com, TwistedOldTales.com (revised, funnified fairy tales) and a large selection of her most important books at AngelaTreatLyonBOOKS.com, and at ColoringBookQueen.com.

More Coloring Goodies by Angela: if you like coloring these mandalas, you'll also like coloring the journal covers, laptop skins, pillows, tote bags and other marvelous things Angela has designed with her mandalas. Search out the **Color Me Collection** at RedBubble.com.

Even More Goodies: you'll love coloring the individual 8.5" x 11" and the 11" x 14" poster pages, and the sets of 3 and 5 pages. Just look for **Angela Treat Lyon** and **ColoringBookQueen** on Etsy.com.

Horses!

Why Horses? Because I love them.

Simple as that. And millions of others, do, too. Horses mean freedom, fun, excitement, speed, beauty, elegance, dignity...and did I mention freedom? Who can look at a herd of wild horses galloping across the plains and not think of the feel of the wind in their hair, the strength and power surging through them, the knowledge of freedom in their very cells?!? They are such magnificent animals, each and every one.

You'll find 15 horse images here—well, 14 horses and one zebra—how could I resist?— both simple and complex.

Every page has a blank back so you can color each mandala without bleeding through to the next design. I have signed my name to each image in light grey, so you can sign your own right next to it in partnership.

These designs are great for rank beginners all the way to experts colorists. Feel free to do shading and improvising at whim! All of them are hand drawn. Yes, some of the lines are a little wobbly—years of using power sculpture tools has left me with a slight tremor in my hands.

I purposely left unfinished lines and open shapes in the designs so you can have fun making your own completions using shading, lines, dots, circles and shapes as you add your own individual touch.

Have a blast with these—and remember to break the Fun Meter!

Much aloha to you -

Angela

Table of Contents

Created with love for my grand-daughter, Ava.

Buddies

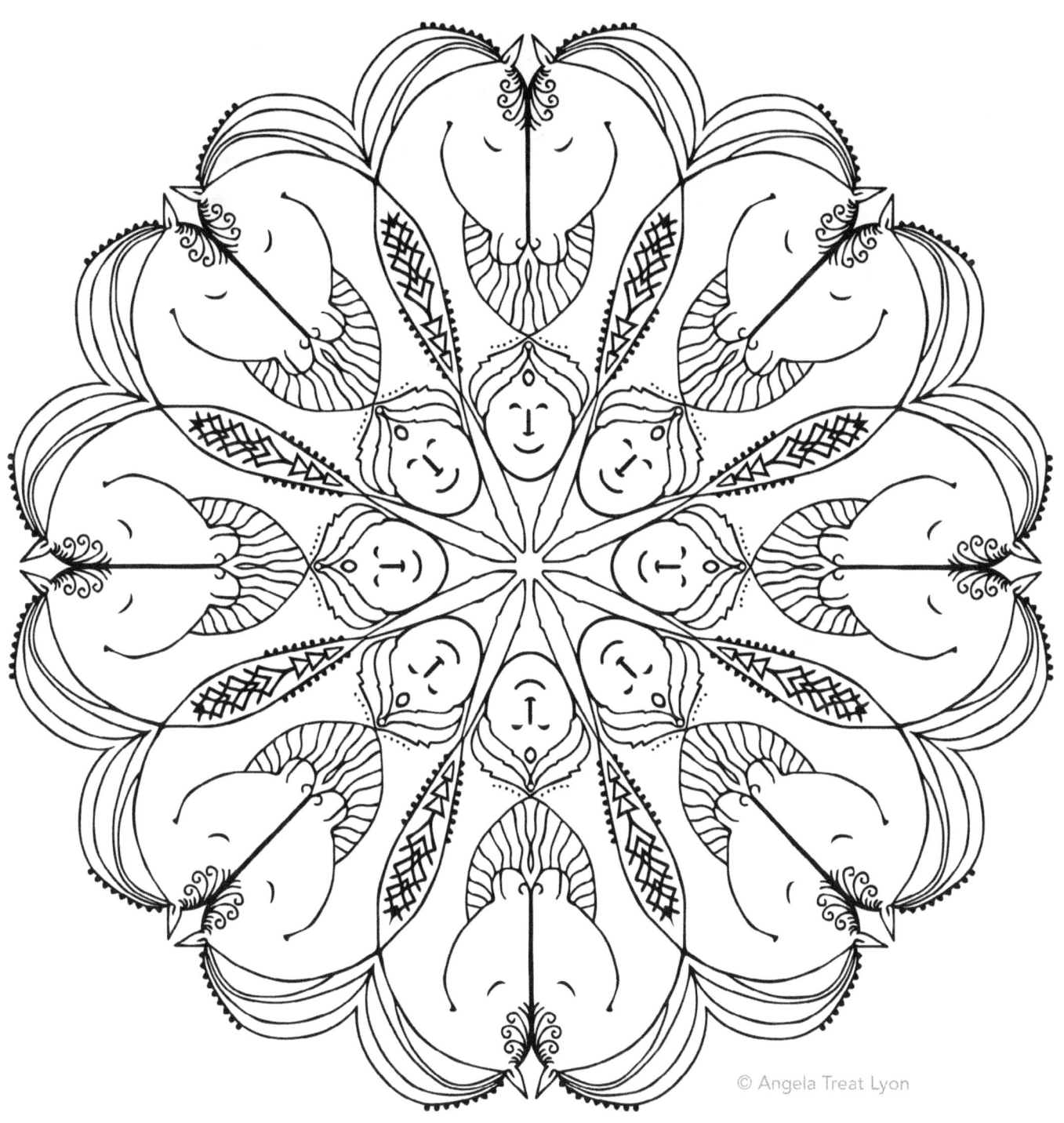

© Angela Treat Lyon

Fountain of Horses

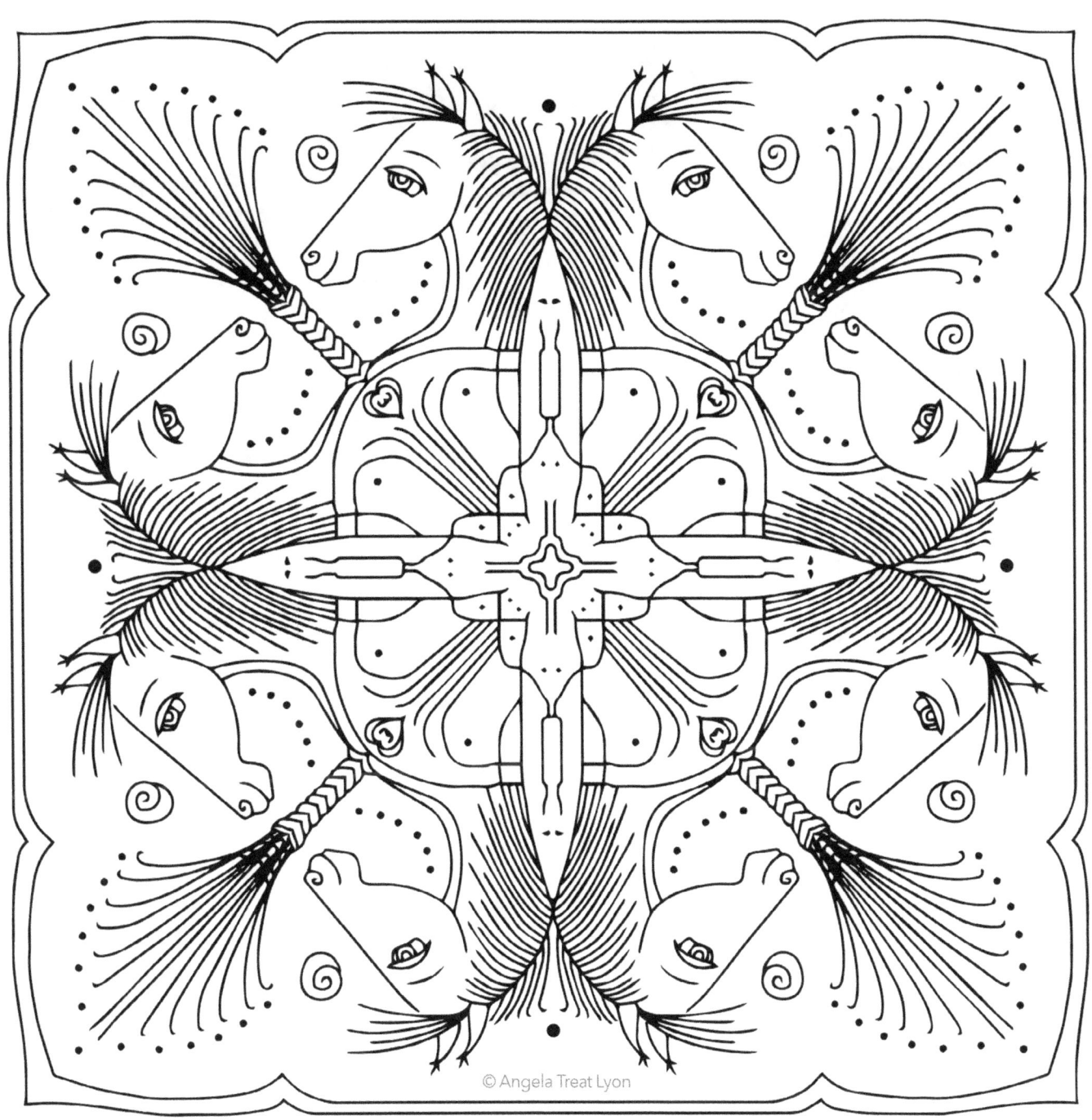

© Angela Treat Lyon

Wild Mustangs

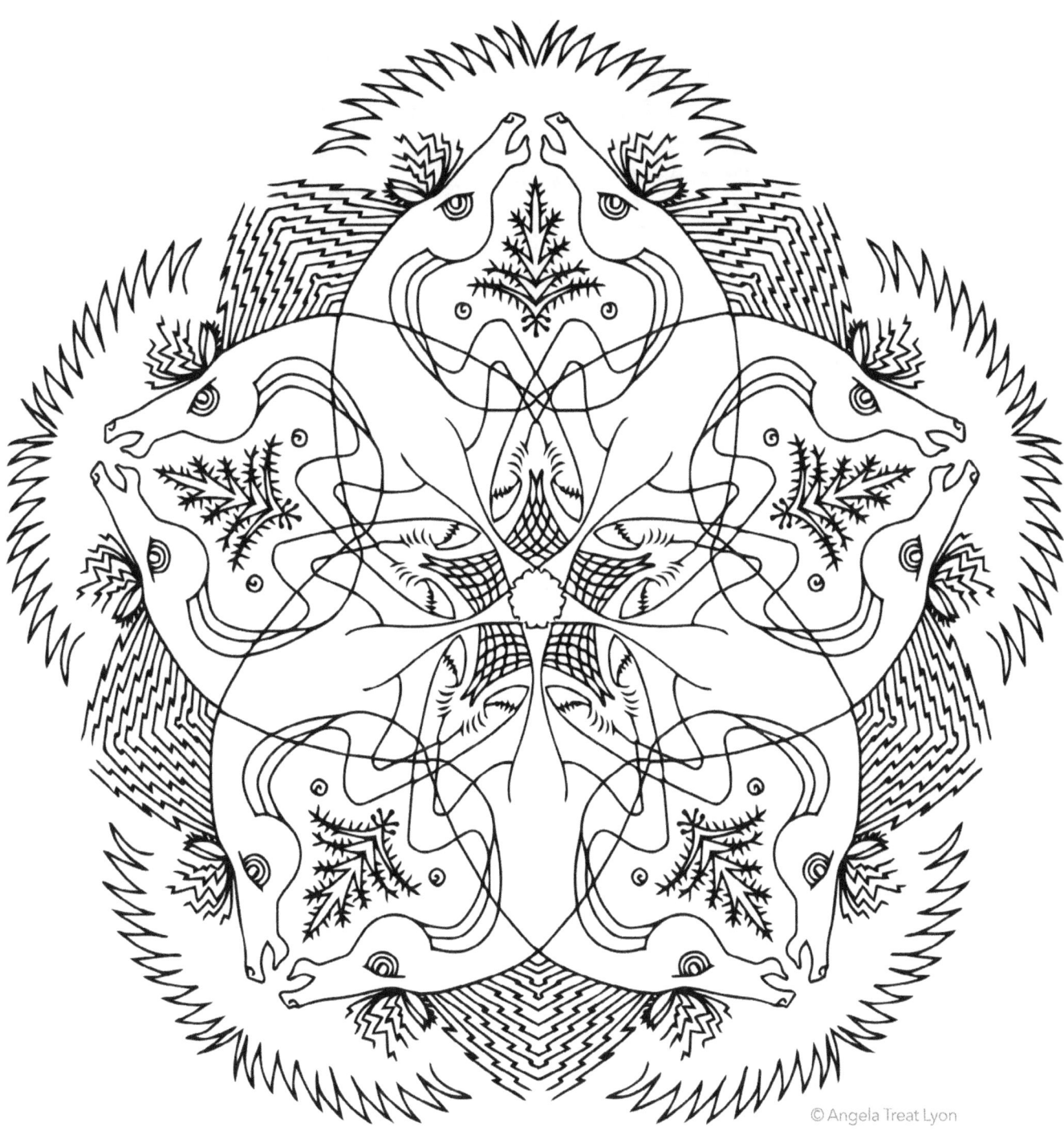

© Angela Treat Lyon

Moon Horses

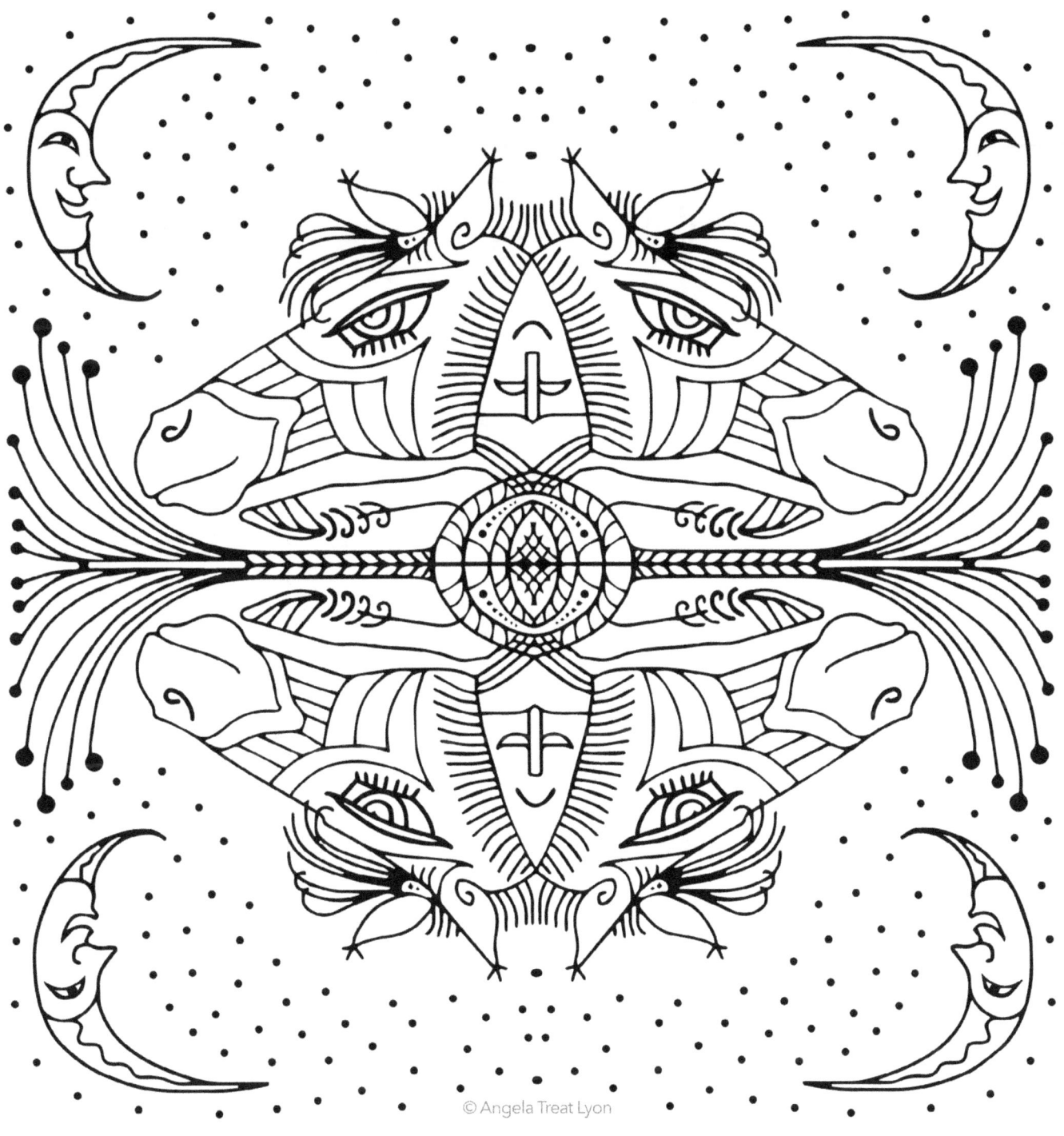

© Angela Treat Lyon

Rainbow Race

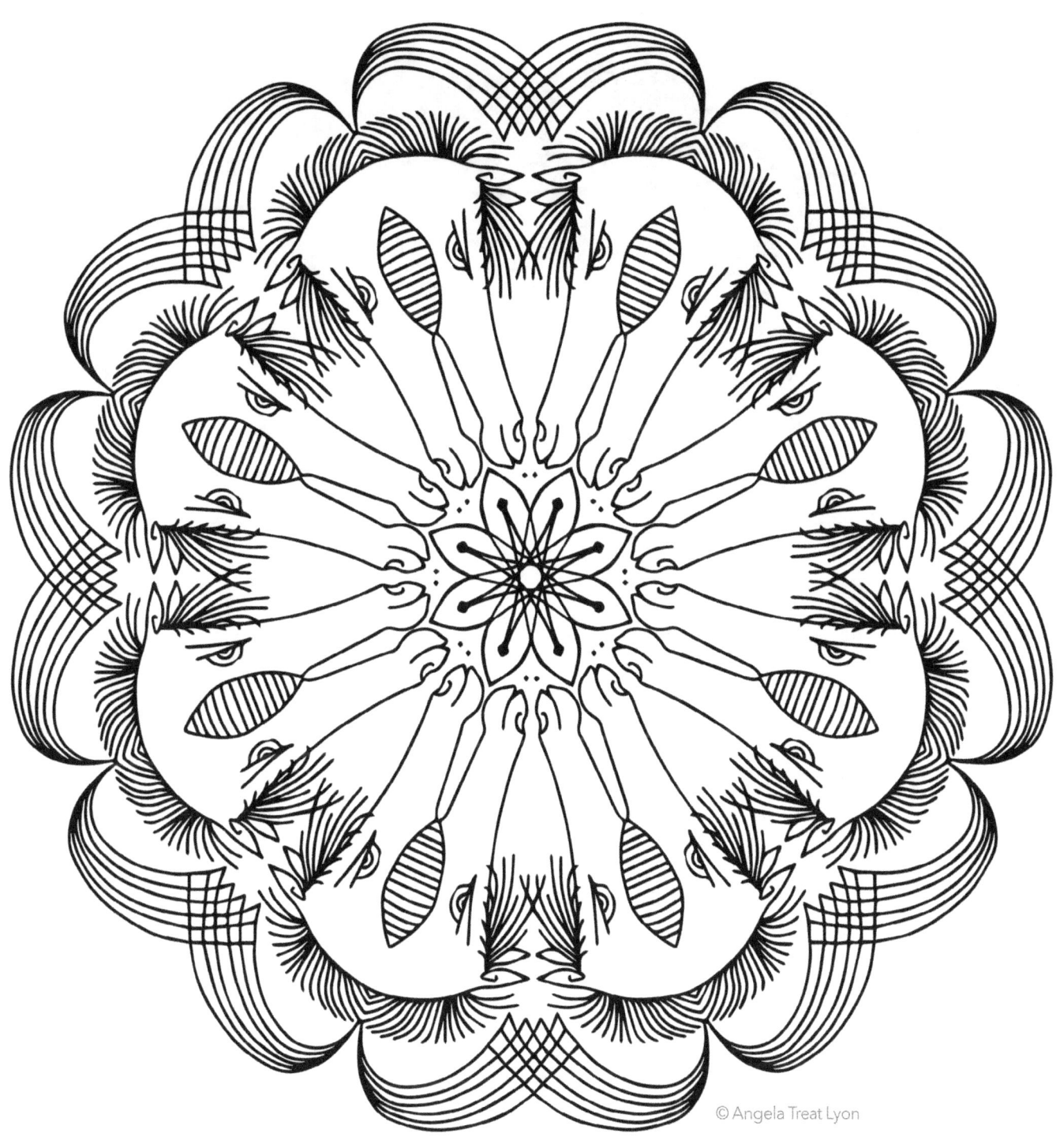

© Angela Treat Lyon

Howling

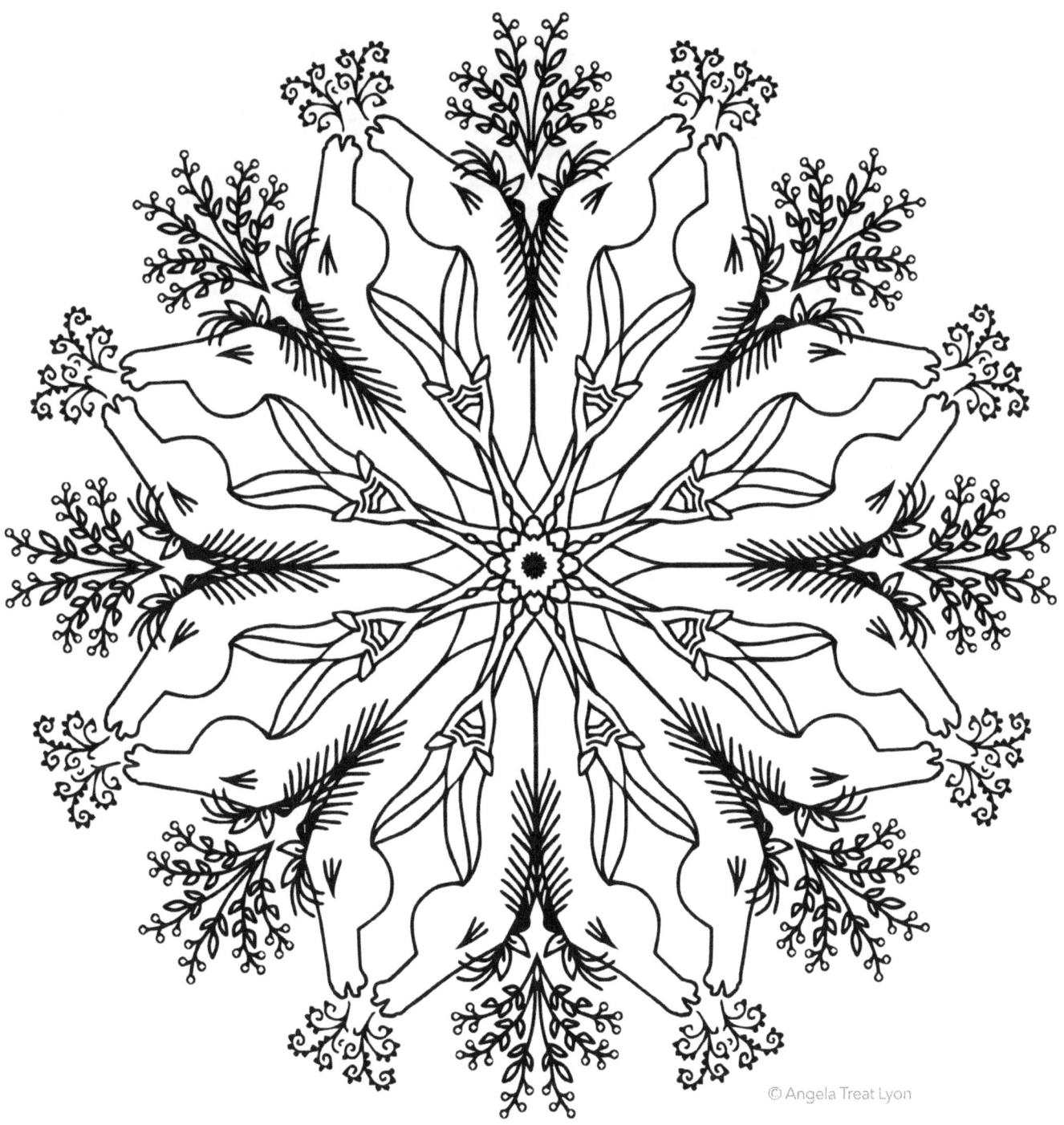

© Angela Treat Lyon

Intent

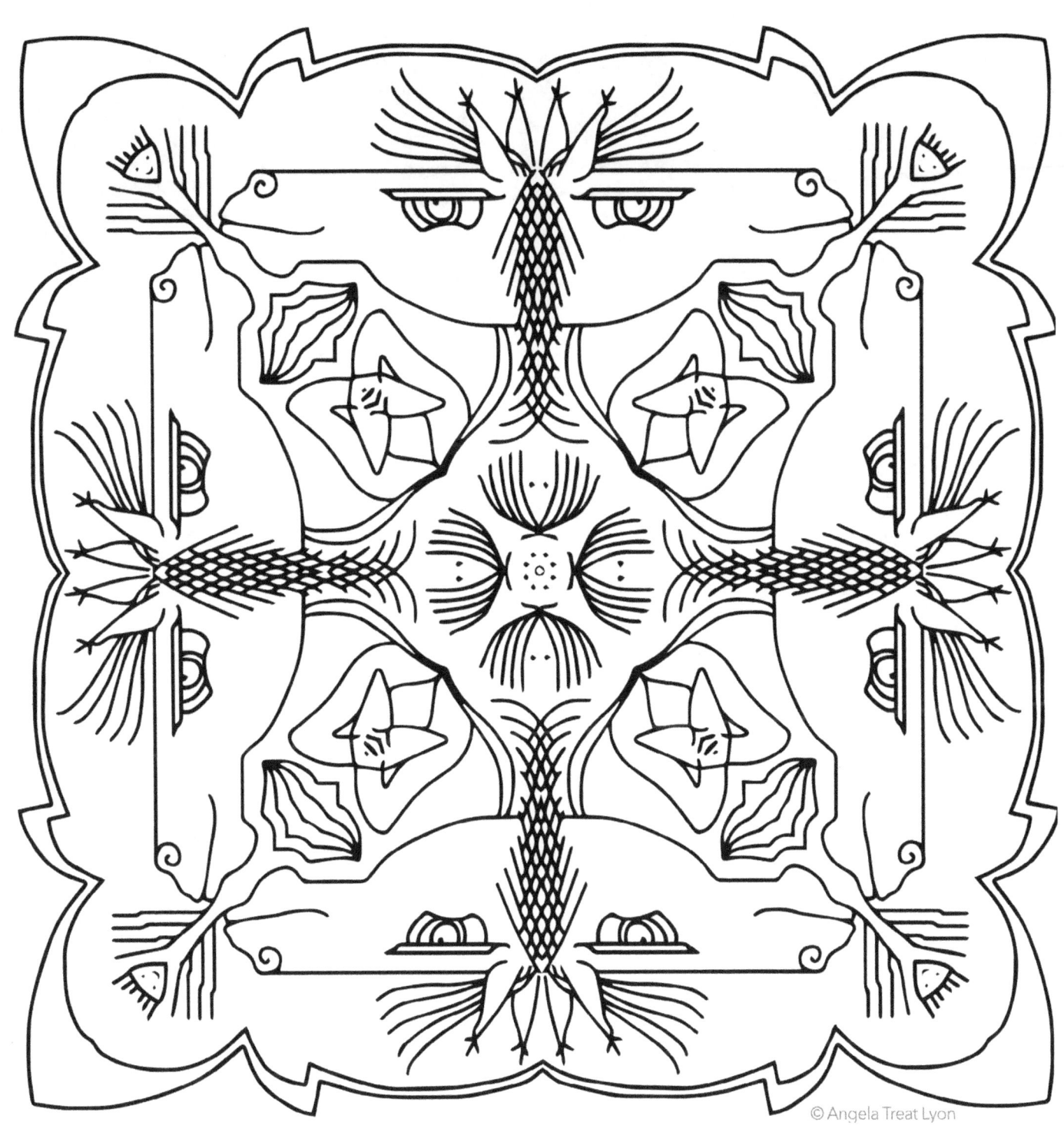

Family Crest

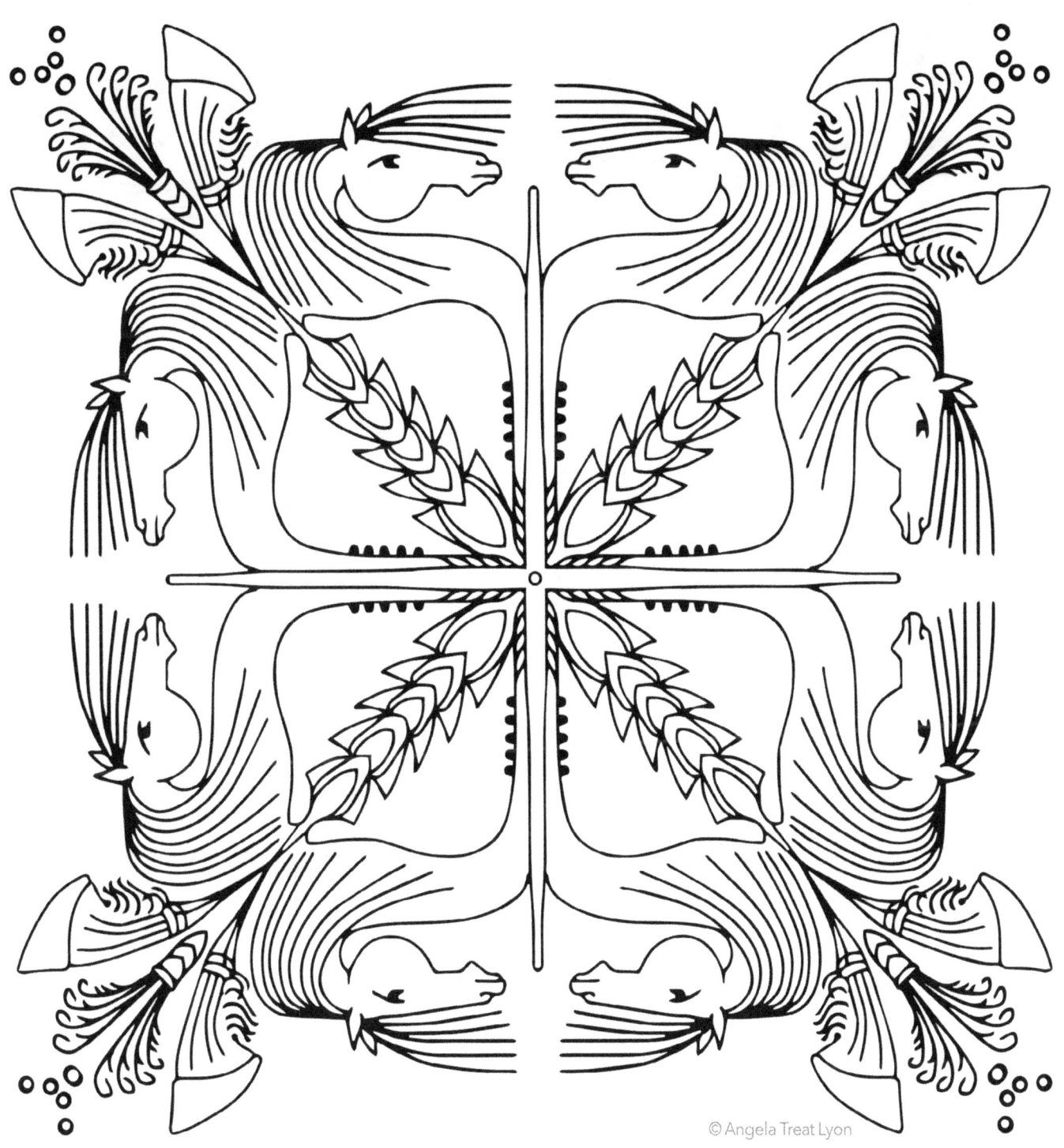

Hoofshake

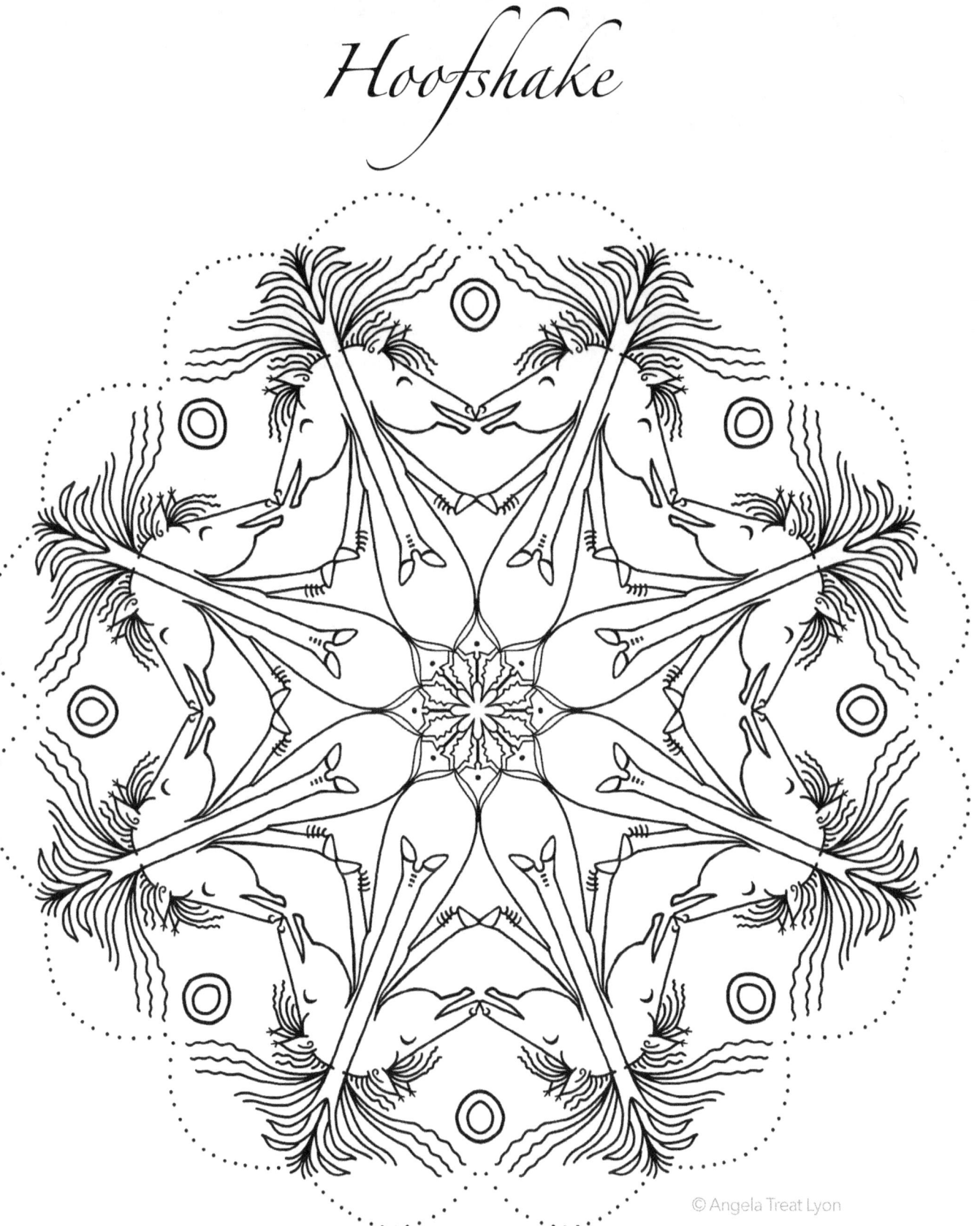

© Angela Treat Lyon

Dignified

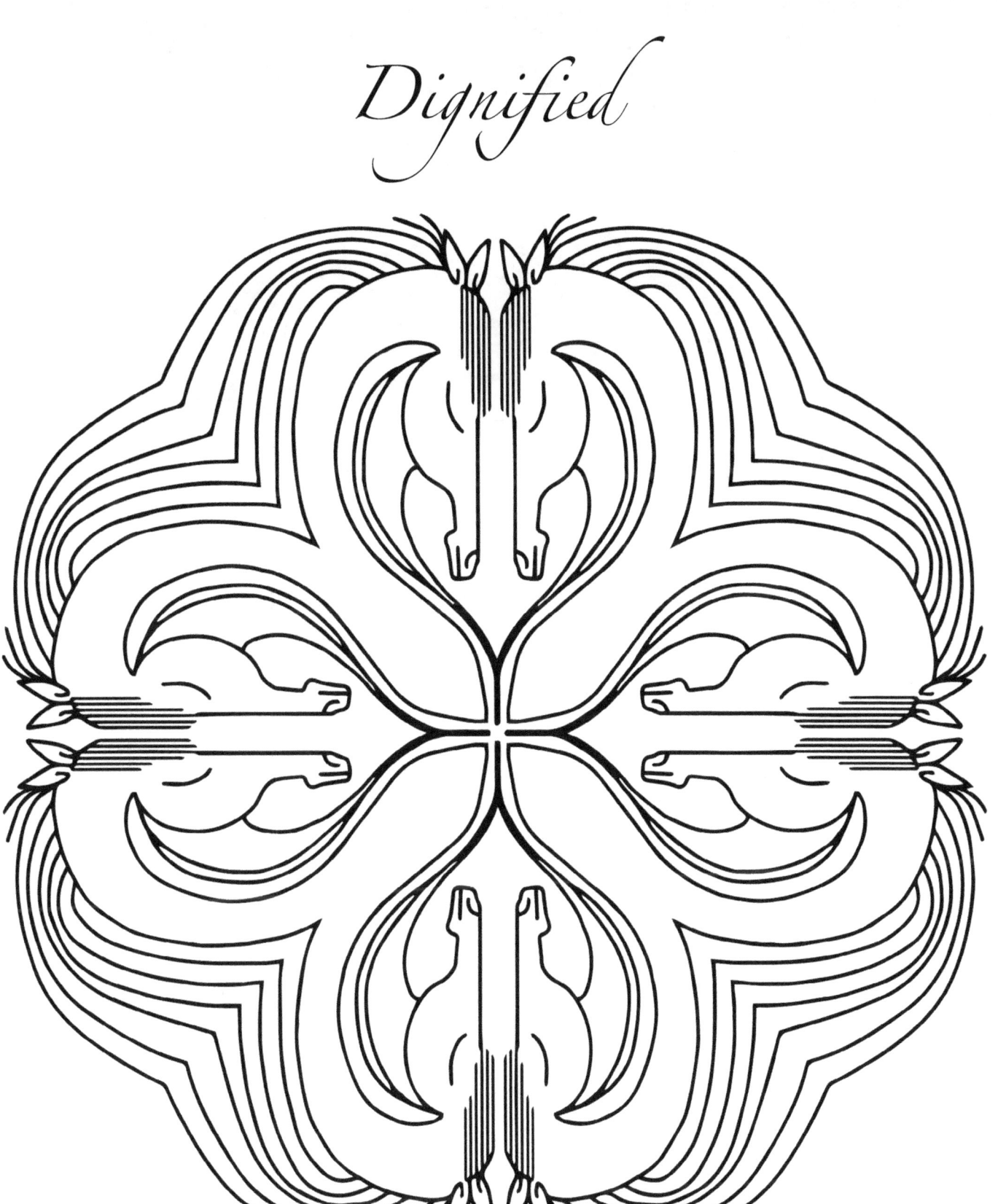

© Angela Treat Lyon

Under the Horse Star

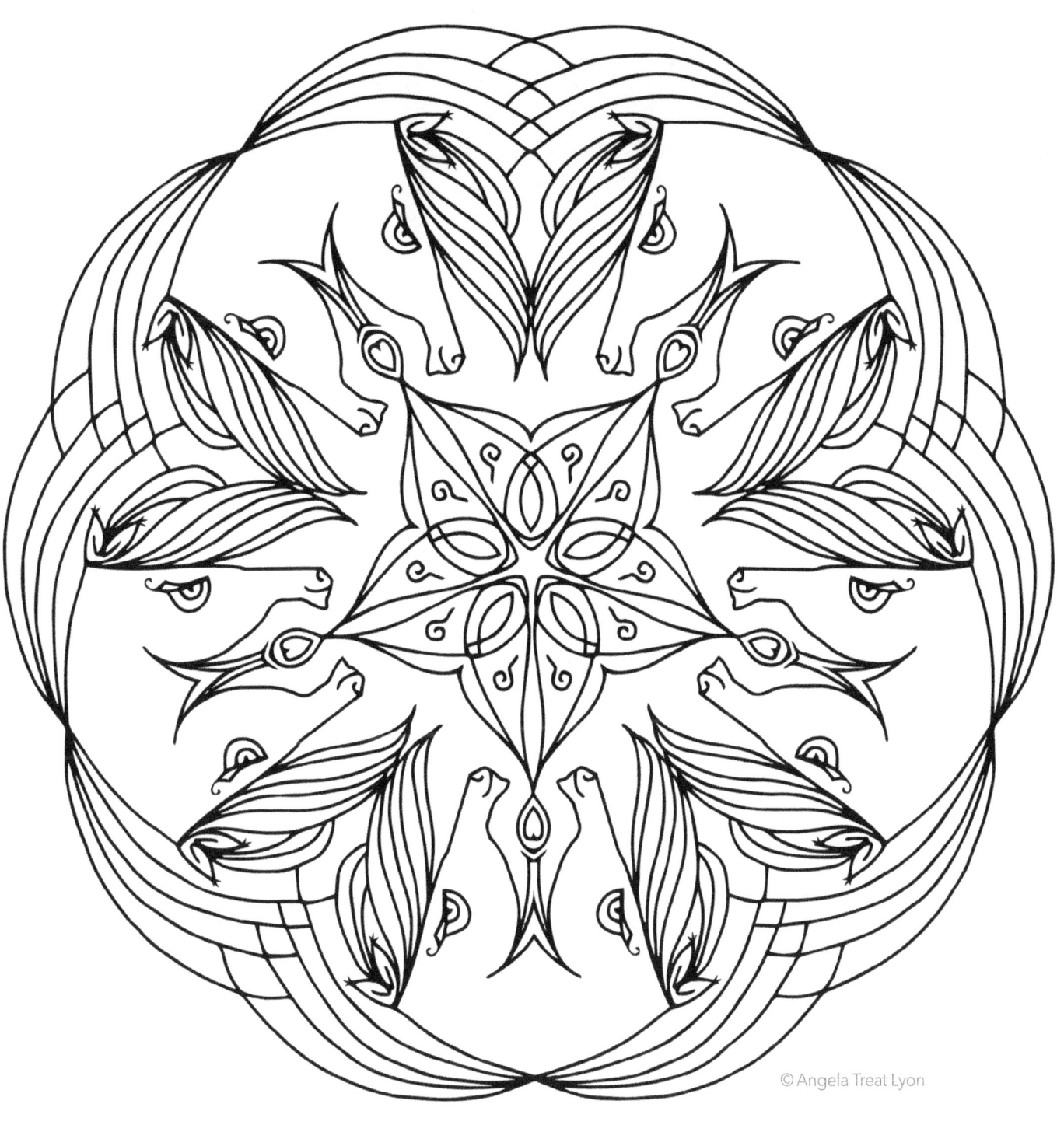

© Angela Treat Lyon

Handsome

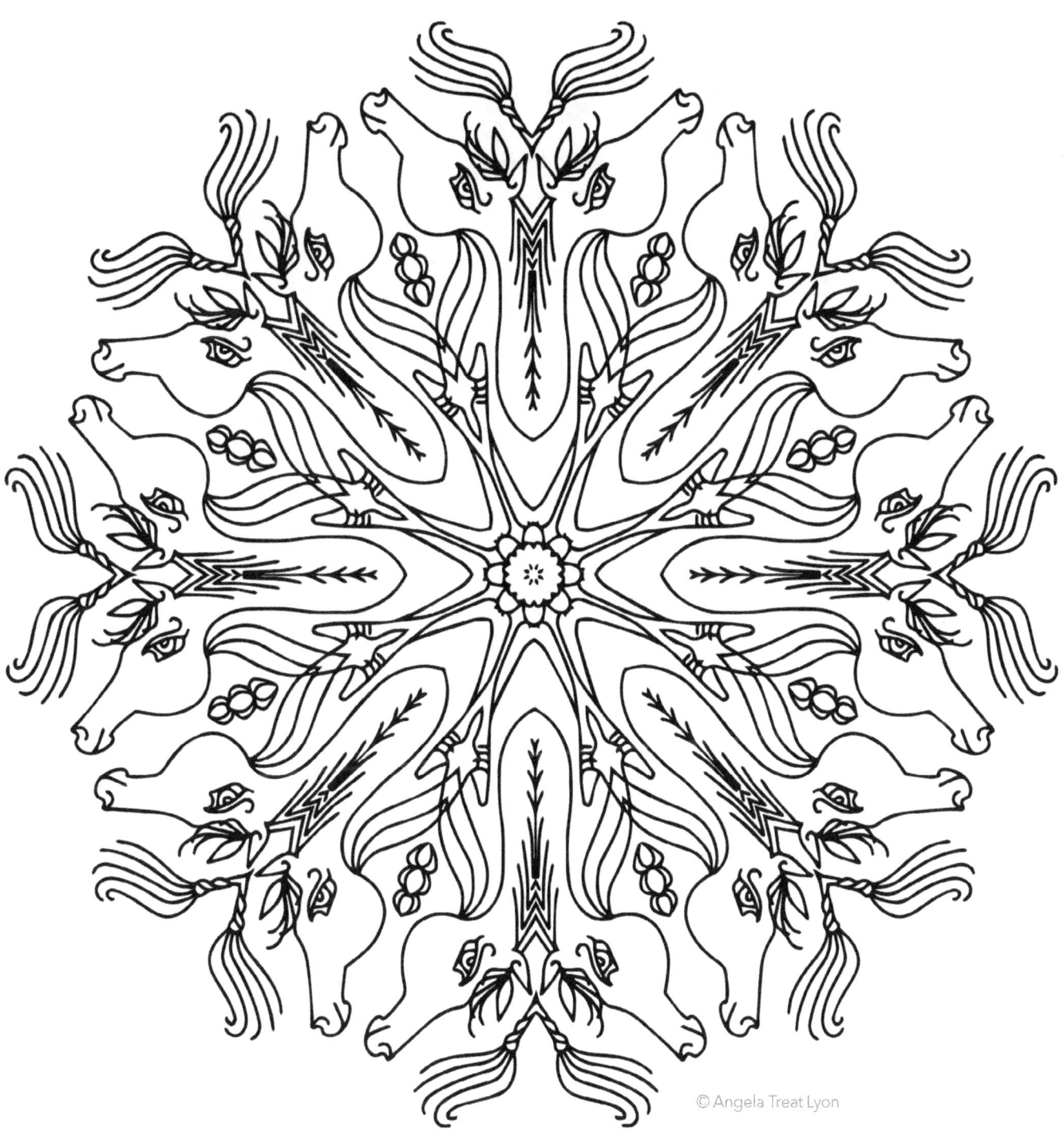

© Angela Treat Lyon

Zig Zag Zebras

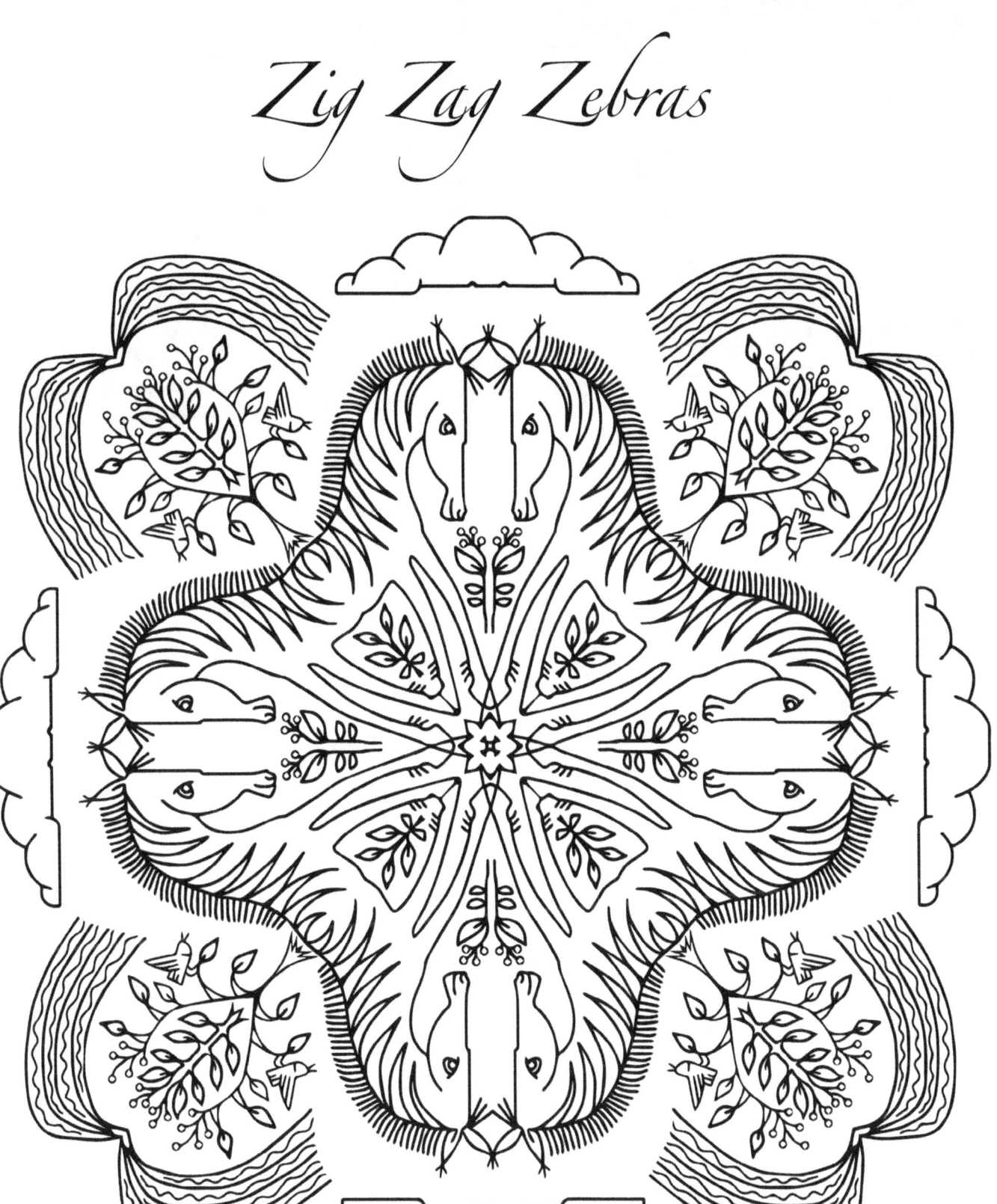

© Angela Treat Lyon

Happy

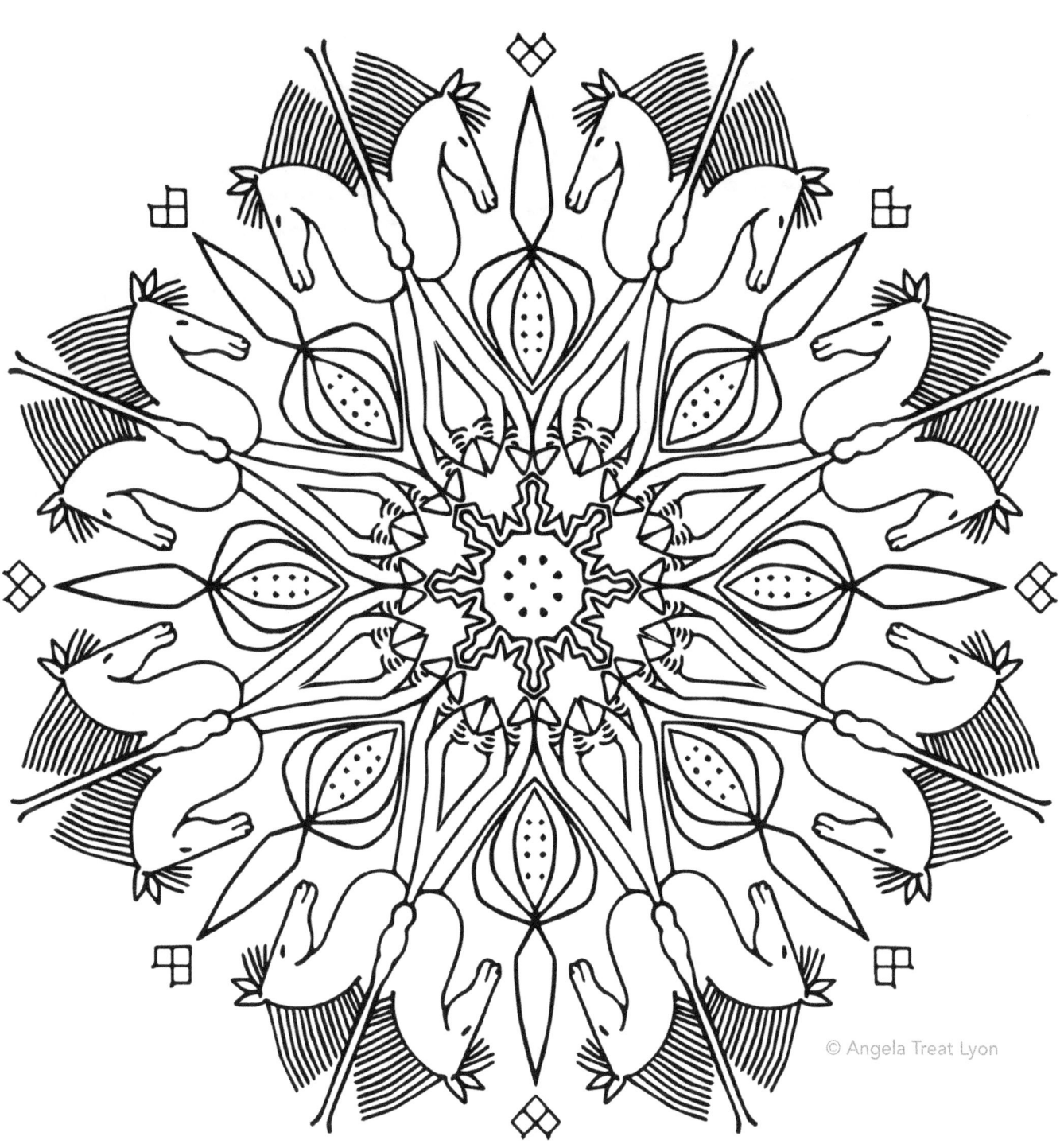

© Angela Treat Lyon

Horse Play

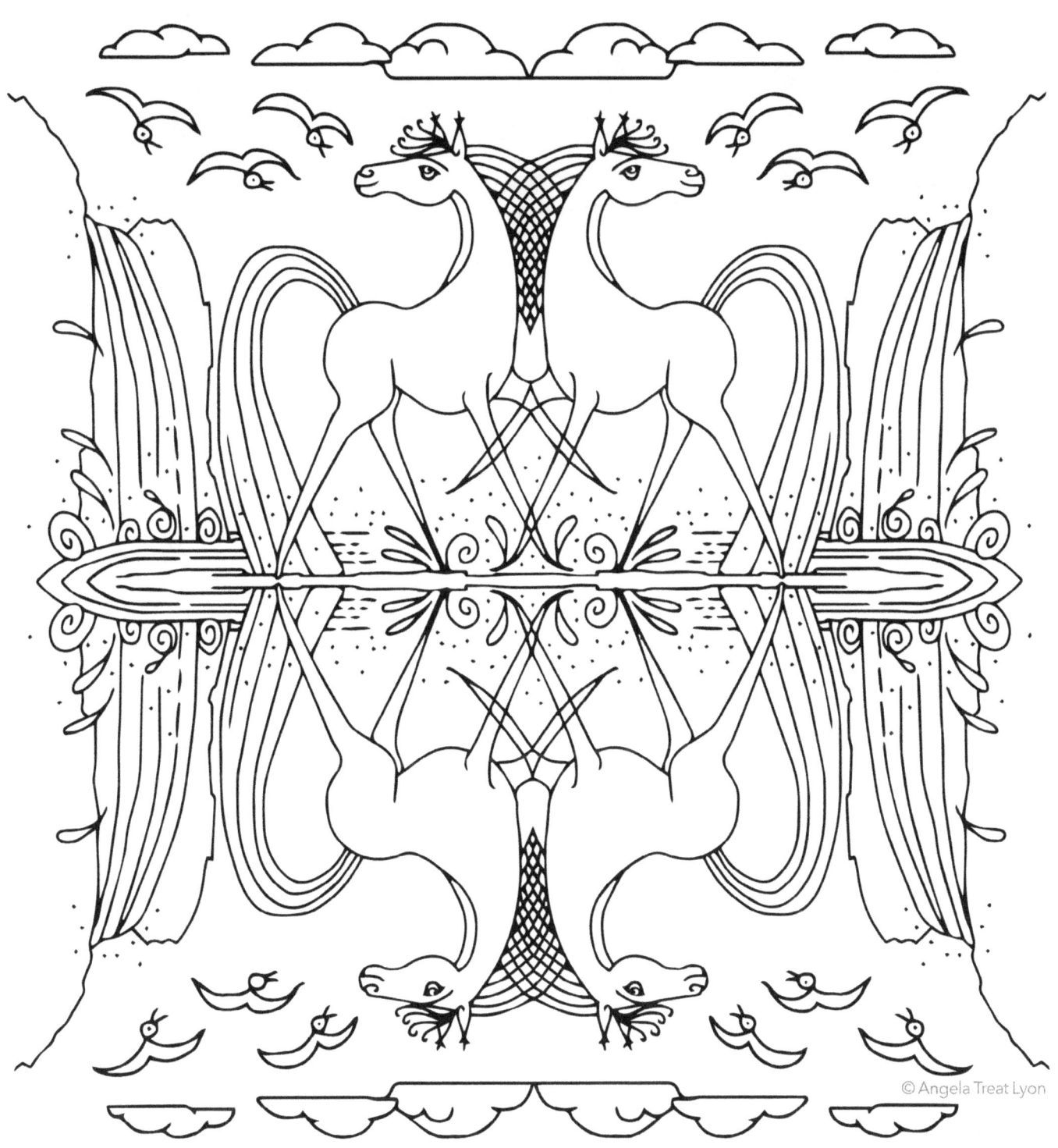

© Angela Treat Lyon

More Books by Angela Treat Lyon: on Amazon.com, TwistedOldTales.com (revised, funnified fairy tales) and a large selection of her most important books at AngelaTreatLyonBOOKS.com, and at ColoringBookQueen.com.

More Coloring Goodies by Angela: if you like coloring these mandalas, you'll also like coloring the journal covers, laptop skins, pillows, tote bags and other marvelous things Angela has designed with her mandalas. Search out the Color Me Collection at RedBubble.com.

Even More Goodies: you'll love coloring the individual 8.5" x 11" and the 11" x 14" poster pages, and the sets of 3 and 5 pages. Just look for **Angela Treat Lyon** and **ColoringBookQueen** on Etsy.com.

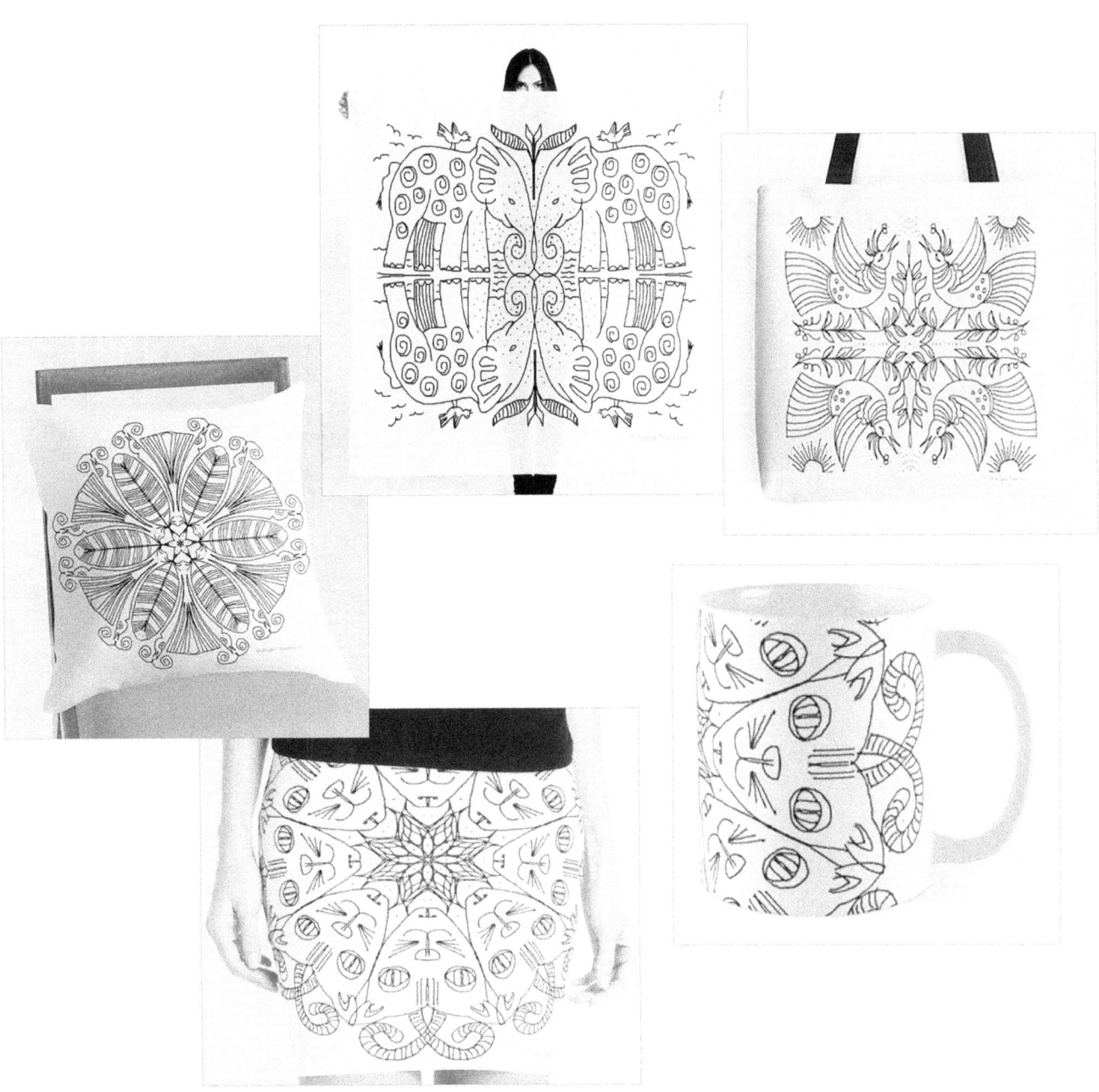

Much aloha to you...

I hope you've had fun playing with these designs. Stay tuned, because I'm making new and different designs all the time!

I invite you to check out more of my artwork (contemporary abstract and stylized figurative oil paintings, gem-colored alcohol paintings and stone sculpture) at AngelaTreatLyonART.com, and more of my books on Amazon, EFTBooks.com, TwistedOldTales.com and AngelaTreatLyonBOOKS.com. And, of course more coloring books at ColoringBookQueen.com (including my new erotic ones).

My best aloha to you -

Angela